WHY SETTLE FOR A SLICE, WHEN YOU CAN HAVE THE WHOLE PIE!

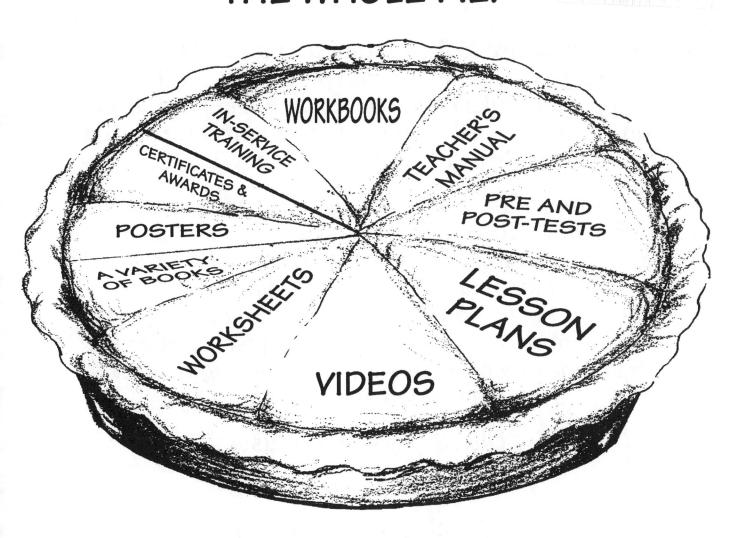

The workbooks are designed for K-12 and are a very important component of SETCLAE's comprehensive, Africentric, multicultural curriculum.

ACKNOWLEDGMENTS

I give all praise to the Creator and special thanks to my family, extended and otherwise, for their support. Thanks to Jawanza, for having the vision and insight to believe that we could produce such a comprehensive curriculum as SETCLAE.

Thanks to the entire African American Images family for their patience while I completed this project. Most of all, thanks to those third graders in my life who help me think like them and inspire me to learn as I teach. Finally, thanks to my own fourth grader, Yakini, whose third grade memories were very helpful in creating activities that you will learn from and enjoy!

Give thanks and praise.

Asante Sana

(Thank You Very Much)

Sister Folami

SETCLAE
Self-Esteem Through Culture Leads to
Academic Excellence
3rd Grade Workbook

Harambee Sessions Illustrations provided by Reginald Mackey

First edition

Second printing

Copyright © 1993 by Folami Prescott, M.A. and Jawanza Kunjufu, Ph.D.

Kiswahili for Dependable & Cheerful

African American Images

Chicago, Illinois

THE SETCLAE WORKBOOK
THIRD GRADE
TABLE OF CONTENTS

INTRODUCTION

HARAMBEE SESSIONS

INTRODUCTION

You will address the meaning of your favorite songs, relationships with your friends and family, your feelings about school, what it means to be a man or a woman, and some very important, enlightening lessons regarding African and African American history and culture.

Our concern for you will become very clear as you continue to use this workbook. It offers a great deal of activities, exercises, and ideas for you to use and share with others. In fact, working with others is the name of the game in SETCLAE. Working in Harambee Groups (Harambee means "Let's pull together" in Kiswahili), you, your peers and family members (extended and otherwise) will learn, sing, learn, dance, learn, act, write, learn, discuss, think, and grow as you explore some of the most critical issues concerning and affecting our families and communities.

For each Harambee Time, there are a number of activities. On each page, we list the materials you will need, topics for discussion and writing and an activity that gets the family and community involved. The Harambee Group symbol (HG) which is adjacent to the word Materials, lets you know you will be working with your Harambee Group for that session.

To get the full benefits from this workbook, you will be using it as just one component of the SETCLAE program. If you are using it exclusively, you will need to have the following books and materials to complete the activities:

Lessons From History *(Elementary)* by Dr. Jawanza Kunjufu *(book and videotape)*

Sparkle by Sadie Turner Pitts

Carla and Annie by Susan K. Smith

The Best Face of All by Wilesse Comissiong

There are other publications and audio-visuals that would be helpful but are not absolutely necessary. However, we hope you will utilize your resources (libraries, schools, videotape collection, friends,etc.) as well as continue to build your own library of African and African American History and Culture.

There is one thing you <u>must</u> do before you go any further:

Let your **KUUMBA** (creativity) flow!!!

Enjoying the Benefits of SETCLAE

Here are some tips to help you enjoy the benefits of SETCLAE:

1. **Be an active Harambee Group member!** Complete the assignments. Ask questions. Help members of the group who don't work as quickly as yourself.

2. **Be creative!** When coloring materials are needed, use a variety including markers, paints, crayons, tissue paper, whatever you can get your hands on.

3. **Be resourceful!** Use magazines such as *Ebony, Essence, Jet, YSB, The Source, Emerge, African Commentary, Black Enterprise,* and other publications. They are filled with relevant information, lessons from history, and illustrations of Black life.

4. **Be original!** Use your ideas to create poems, raps, skits, songs, dances, dramatic presentations, speeches, plays, books, articles, and letters to share your insight with others.

5. **Be encouraging!** When working in Harambee Groups, encourage members to take on tasks according to talents and interests. Each group should identify someone to fulfill the following roles:

Moderator
Timekeeper
Reporter
Recorder
Illustrator
Rapper / Poet
Observer

Of course, one person can perform several of these roles simultaneously.

6. Always remember: everyone is a "mwalimu mwanafunzi" (teacher and student).

7. Never forget what SETCLAE stands for:
   Self-Esteem Through Culture Leads to Academic Excellence!!!

Correlation of SETCLAE Lessons to Academic Objectives

In an effort to accommodate the implementation of SETCLAE into the existing curriculum in your school, the Harambee Time sessions have been correlated to the most common academic objectives for this grade level. The *Typical Course of Study* for kindergarten through twelfth grade was compiled by World Book Educational Products. Curriculum materials such as *The Nault-Caswell-Brain Analysis of Courses of Study* and others from The National Council of Teachers of Mathematics, English, and Social Studies were analyzed in the preparation of the study guide.

Please use this guide to help give SETCLAE a home in your setting. You will soon see that the program is a welcome and valuable member of the family and HARAMBEE TIME can be effective in "pulling us together" as we build Tomorrow's Leaders. We also encourage you to incorporate the learning and classroom management styles (e.g. student-made materials and Harambee groups respectively) used in SETCLAE into all subjects taught. And share your success stories with your colleagues!

LA-Language Arts
SS-Social Studies
HT-Health
MT-Mathematics

1 - Let Me Introduce Myself
LA Note taking
    Report writing

2 - Bonding
LA Note taking
    Research
    Listening and speech activities
    Collective decision making

3 - Rules, Rights and Responsibilities
LA Deductive Reasoning

4 - We Like That!
LA Collective decision making
    Listening / spelling

5 - Goal Setting

    LA Writing skills

        Using magazines

6 - I Can Be!

    LA Career Education

        Using basic reference materials

7 - Me and My Family

    SS U.S. Geography

        Our Native background

8 - Names We Call Ourselves

    LA Writing skills

        Extended vocabulary

        Our American culture

9 - The Color Question

    LA Writing skills

        Extended vocabulary

        Listening and speech

10 - *Lessons* Video with Dr. Jawanza Kunjufu

    LA Critique

    SS Our American culture

    HT Type and functions of food

        Body's utilization of food

11- Africa, The Continent

    SS Map and globe Skills

        Our Native background

        Exploration and Discovery

    LA Creative Dramatics

        Reading non-fiction

12 - Egypt is in Africa!

    SS Our Native background

    LA Literal and Inferential Reading Skills

22 - How I Spend My Time
LA Critical Thinking

23 - Television
LA Deductive reasoning

24 - Values
LA Deductive reasoning

25 - Advertising Images
LA Report writing skills
Critical Thinking skills

26 - School!!
LA Creative writing skills

27 - Me and My Friends
LA Creative dramatics
Critical Thinking skills
Listening and speech activities

28 - How to Say No
LA Creative dramatics
Problem Solving

29 - The Nguzo Saba
LA Value Development
SS Our American culture

30 - Kuumba Means Creativity
SS Community empowerment

31 - Carla and Annie
LA Critical Thinking skills

32- Becoming a Man or Woman
HT Male/Female Sexuality
LA Deductive reasoning

SETCLAE Vocabulary Means WORD POWER!

There is power in having an extensive (look that word up!) vocabulary. Look up the definitions for these words and write a sentence (or two) for each word. Also, on a separate sheet of paper, write a sentence on how the word is used in the Harambee Time listed. Then use these words everyday!

Don't forget, you lose what you don't use!

Harambee Time #2
activity

Harambee Time #14
resist

Harambee Time #15
privilege
boycott

Harambee Time #16
relevant

Harambee Time #17
politics
community

Harambee Time #19
dialect

Harambee Time #22
monitor

Harambee Time #24
value

Harambee Time #25
advertising
purpose

Harambee Time #29
self-determination
cooperative
economics

The SETCLAE Student Profile (3rd Grade)

Instructions

Please answer the following questions on the answer sheet and think real hard about how you really feel before answering each one. THERE ARE NO RIGHT OR WRONG ANSWERS. We want YOUR answers.

Part I

Read each statement or question. If it is true for you, circle the answer "a" on the answer sheet. If it is not true for you, circle the answer "b". Answer every question even if it's hard to decide. (Just think about yourself and what's important to you.) Select only one answer for each question. Write on the answer sheet only.

1. I like to be alone sometimes.   a. Yes   b. No

2. I like to stand in front of the class and speak.   a. Yes   b. No

3. When we are cleaning up our classroom, if I finish before everybody else, I play.   a. Yes   b. No

4. School will help me to be what I want to be.   a. Yes   b. No

5. If I can't think of anything good to say about someone, I don't say anything at all.   a. Yes   b. No

6. I know what kind of person I want to be when I grow up.   a. Yes   b. No

7. I like to play with my favorite toy all by myself more than I like to share it with others.   a. Yes   b. No

8. If things don't go my way, I get mad.   a. Yes   b. No

9. School is boring most of the time.   a. Yes   b. No

10. Do you speak slang and
    Standard English?   a. Yes   b. No

11. If I don't see a trash can, I throw my
    trash on the ground.   a. Yes   b. No

12. I like participating in special projects
    like science fairs and spelling bees.   a. Yes   b. No

13. When the truth is hard to say,
    I don't say it.   a. Yes   b. No

14. Would you like to be in a family
    other than your own?   a. Yes   b. No

15. My neighborhood is
    a good place to live.   a. Yes   b. No

16. I can get any job I want, if I work at
    it hard enough.   a. Yes   b. No

17. I like being with people that are
    different from me.   a. Yes   b. No

18. I like me!   a. Yes   b. No
19. Do you believe you can have your own
    business when you get older?   a. Yes   b. No

20. There are a lot of people in the world
    more important than I am.   a. Yes   b. No

21. African Americans only do well in
    sports, music, movies , and TV.   a. Yes   b. No
22. If I could, I would make friends with
    races of all people.   a. Yes   b. No

23. In my opinion, most Black people
    are lazy.   a. Yes   b. No

24. I want to be able to speak Standard
    English when I go some places and
    when talking to some people.   a. Yes   b. No.

Part II

Read each item carefully. If it is something that is important to you, select "a" on the answer sheet. If it is not important to you (it doesn't really matter or has nothing to do with you), select "b". Take your time and think about it. There are no right or wrong answers. We want to know your feelings.

1. Helping others

        a. Important to Me   b. Not Important to Me

2. What others think of me

        a. Important to Me   b. Not Important to Me

3. Reading

        a. Important to Me   b. Not Important to Me

4. Television

        a. Important to Me   b. Not Important to Me

5. Solving problems by fighting

        a. Important to Me   b. Not Important to Me

6. Learning about my family members - dead & living

        a. Important to Me   b. Not Important to Me

7. Getting along with others

        a. Important to Me   b. Not Important to Me

8. Doing whatever my friends do

        a. Important to Me   b. Not Important to Me

9. Expensive clothes

        a. Important to Me   b. Not Important to Me

10. Doing well in school

        a. Important to Me   b. Not Important to Me

11. Speaking up for myself & my ideas

        a. Important to Me   b. Not Important to Me

12. Being positive most of the time

                        a. Important to Me   b. Not Important to Me

13. Life in Africa today

                        a. Important to Me   b. Not Important to Me

Part III

Read each statement carefully. Read the choices. Then draw a line under each statement that accurately describes you.

1. If asked to describe my personality to someone I'd never met, I would use statements like:

I'm fun to be around.	I like to get in trouble.
I give up easily.	I'm a good fighter.
I'm a leader.	I'm happy.
I like helping others.	I'm slow.
I'm easily bored.	I'm unhappy.
I'm friendly.	I worry a lot.
I'm popular.	I'm big and bad.
I'm outgoing.	

2. If asked to describe my physical appearance, I would say I am or have

average-looking	too short	too fat
pretty eyes	light-skinned	dark-skinned
nice hair	beautiful/handsome	slim
a head that is too big		lips that are too big
a nose that is too big		

3. Circle one.

              I   a. like   my hair.

                          b. don't like

4. I chose the above answer because my hair is:

short	long	thick	straight
curly	nappy	dark	red
light	natural	braided	mine!

5. Circle one.

I   a. like   my skin color.

                      b. don't like

6. I chose the above answer because my skin is:

               dark   light   just right

7. Circle the five words that first come to your mind when you hear the word Africa.

slavery	city
Tarzan	jungle
continent	kings and queens
Egypt	pyramids
civilization	savage
homeland	country
wild	monkeys

8. Circle the one that is more important to you. Choose only one!

I like

a. being popular

b. doing well in school

Part IV

Carefully read the following statements and choices for answers. Then pick the answer that is best for you. Circle the letter that is in front of your answer below.

There are NO RIGHT OR WRONG ANSWERS. Choose the answer that is right for YOU.

1. When my friends have fun without me, I

    a. am happy they are having fun.

    b. don't even think about it.

    c. wish they weren't having fun without me.

2. When I hear something negative about a person, I

    a. can't wait to tell someone else.

    b. talk to the person to see how I can help.

    c. try to find out more.

3. When someone says something about me that is not good but is true, I
    a. get upset.
    b. don't want to be around them anymore.
    c. listen and learn from their observations.
    d. say something about them that is not good.

4. When someone laughs at me,
    a. I get upset.
    b. my feelings are hurt.
    c. I laugh with them.
    d. I make a joke of it.
    e. I don't like it.

5. When I am talking to someone, most of the time I look
    a. at their hands.
    b. into their eyes.
    c. at the floor.
    d. all around.

6. How much time do you spend making yourself look good?
    a. no time
    b. very little time
    c. some of the time
    d. all of the time

7. If I had lots of money, I would
    a. be happy all the time.
    b. help others.
    c. need and want more money.
    d. save it.

8. When I play team games, I
    a. like to be the captain.
    b. have fun even if my team loses.
    c. don't like losing.
    d. often get in a fight.

9. When I need help, I
    a. get frustrated.
    b. ask for it.
    c. try to figure it out myself.

10. I pick my friends because
   a. they look good.
   b. they are cool.
   c. we can talk a lot.
   d. they give me things.

11. I am glad I am the race I am.
   a. Yes
   b. No

12. I chose the answer above because
   a. I am proud of it.
   b. I know my history.
   c. it sounds good.
   d. I was taught by my family.
   e. my friends chose the same answer.

13. My favorite musical group or person is _____ because
   a. they play good dancing music.
   b. they sing about good things.
   c. they make good videos.
   d. of the cursing in the songs.
   e. they play nice music to listen to.

14. A boy becomes a man when
   a. he can handle drugs and crime.
   b. he makes a baby.
   c. he takes care of himself and his family.
   d. he can fight.

15. When I can sit wherever I want in class, I sit
   a. in the middle.
   b. in the front.
   c. in the back.

16. When the teacher leaves the room, I
   a. talk.
   b. stop doing my work.
   c. look at who is being out of order.
   d. find something quiet to do once I finish my work.

17. My favorite TV show is _____ because
    a. it's funny.
    b. there's a lot of kissing/fighting.
    c. I like the nice clothes, fancy cars, and pretty houses.
    d. I learn new things from it.
    e. I like the actors.

18. When I want to do something new (like join a sports team), I
    a. ask my parents to get me started.
    b. plan how I will do it.
    c. just think about it real hard.
    d. ask my friends to get me started.

19. When I do poorly on my schoolwork, I
    a. don't really care.
    b. know I tried my best.
    c. know I should try harder.
    d. know it's only because I can't do any better.
    e. know the teacher gave us work that was too hard or boring.

20. If I could change one thing about myself, it would
    be_____.

21. The thing I like most about myself
    is_____.

22. Answering these questions was
    a. very enjoyable.
    b. no big deal.
    c. a good way to take a closer look at my personal development.
    d. a waste of time.

MATERIALS:

✓ Pencil/Pen
✓ Index Cards

STEPS TO TAKE:

Think of a time that you did something well that would make an interesting news story. Use these questions to help you prepare your top story on the news. Make sure your oral presentation is no longer than two minutes.

WRITE IT DOWN:

How did the experience you described above make you feel about yourself and the others that were there?

_____
_____
_____
_____
_____
_____
_____
_____
_____
_____

LET ME INTRODUCE MYSELF!

THE TOP STORY ON THE NEWS TONIGHT!

Where did it happen?

_____
_____
_____
_____
_____

Who was there?

_____
_____
_____
_____

When did it happen?

_____
_____
_____
_____

How did it happen?

_____
_____
_____
_____

What actually happened?

_____
_____
_____
_____

During the situation, what did you perform very well?

_____
_____
_____
_____

Use an index card to make your own I.D. card. It should look like this:

WHO AM I?

Name _____

Address _____

City, State, Zip _____

Two Things I Like About Myself _____

_____

Something I Do Well _____

_____

MATERIALS (HG)

✓ Poster Board

✓ Coloring Materials

STEPS TO TAKE:

Working in your Harambee Group, select a name for the group on which everyone can agree. Your group will pick a name from one of the five groups listed. For more information on groups 2,3, and 4, see Something You Should Know.

WRITE IT DOWN:

Why is it important to work in groups? In which activities do adults work in groups?

_____
_____
_____
_____
_____
_____
_____
_____
_____
_____
_____

BONDING

CHOOSE FROM:

#1 Lions, Tigers, Bears, Giraffes, Zebras

#2 Nigeria, Kenya, Egypt, Azania, Tanzania (use encyclopedias)

#3 Ashanti, Pondo, Fanti, Ikoma, Chagga (use the book Ashanti to Zulu)

#4 Morehouse Coll., Hampton Univ., Spelman Coll., Tuskegee Inst., Howard Univ.

#5 Scientists, Lawyers, Artists, Teachers, Farmers

In the box below the name, draw a picture of what you think of when you say each name. After the group discusses everyone's drawings and you select one name for the group, use poster board to make a flag for the group. Be sure to creatively write the name of the group and the names of everyone in the group on the flag.

1.	4.
2.	5.
3.	

MATERIALS (HG)

✓ Pencil/Pen

LET'S TALK ABOUT IT

✓ Why do we have rules?

✓ What is a right?

✓ What is a responsibility?

If someone does not meet their responsibilities, what should the consequences be?

A scale is something that is used to balance things as well as to weigh. In ancient Egypt (also known as Kemet), the importance of treating other people right was shown in the symbol of scales called MAAT. In each of the scales shown write one of your rights and the responsibility you must fulfill to earn that right.

WRITE IT DOWN:

We often think of discipline as meaning punishment, but DISCIPLINE MEANS SELF-CONTROL! What do you do that helps you have self-control?

_____

_____

_____

_____

_____

_____

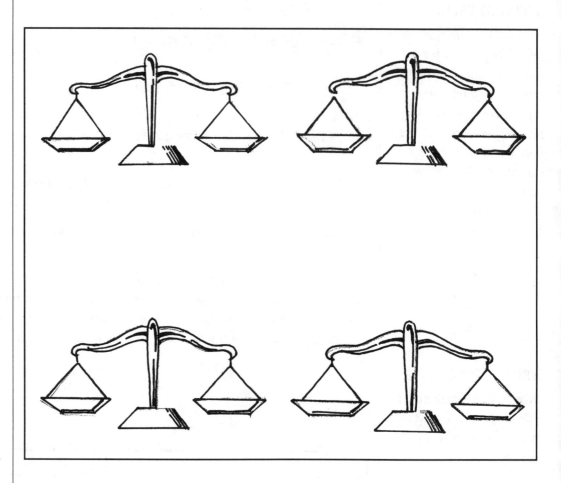

DRAW YOUR OWN SCALE HERE!

MATERIALS (HG)

- ✓ Pencil
- ✓ Coloring Materials
- ✓ Construction Paper
- ✓ Paste
- ✓ Poster Board

STEPS TO TAKE:

Working in your Harambee Group, think of two things you would really like your classmates to do and write them in big letters on strips of construction paper. Two strips from each group will be used to make a poster for the classroom. Glue the strips to a large poster board and write at the top of the poster WE LIKE THAT AND THAT'S THE WAY IT IS.

Use the boxes provided to tell a story about your classmates and the things they do that you like. Draw pictures, too.

WRITE IT DOWN:

Write about someone your age that did something you liked. What did you do to let them know you liked what he or she did?

_____

_____

_____

_____

_____

WE LIKE THAT!

What are some positive things you would like your classmates to do?

1.	2.
3.	4.
5.	6.

MATERIALS

✓ Construction paper
✓ Stapler
✓ Scissors
✓ Paste

HERE ARE SOME IDEAS:

Make your bed every day. Do your homework as soon as you get home. Write a letter to a friend or family member that lives in another state or country. Treat your peers the way you like to be treated (no fighting or name-calling). Meet a new adult friend who can teach you some things.

STEPS TO TAKE:

On a separate sheet of paper, use the following boxes to help you de-scribe your goal and make a book. Number your pages, cut them out, and staple them together.

WRITE IT DOWN:

Name someone you ad-mire who reached a goal. What do you think they had to do to reach that goal?

_____
_____
_____
_____

GOAL SETTING

Think of something you would like to do in one or two months.

Harambee Time #5

1. I Want to...
(Write your goal here. Also draw or cut out pictures to paste in your book.)

_____
_____
_____
_____
_____
_____
_____
_____
_____

2. So I Will.......
(Write the things you must do to meet your goal.)

_____
_____
_____
_____
_____
_____
_____

3. Reaching My Goal
Draw pictures or cut some out of a magazine that show the goal you have set.

4. My Checker Is...(Write the name and phone number of the person who will check on you & your goal.)

_____
_____
_____
_____
_____
_____
_____
_____
_____
_____

MATERIALS (HG)

✓ Reference materials
✓ Scissors
✓ Paste
✓ Pencil

STEPS TO TAKE:

Your group is going to name careers that begin with one of the groups of letters listed: A-E, F-J, K-O, P-T, U-Z. Use magazines, encyclopedias, telephone books, and posters to help you find careers that begin with your five letters. FIND A PICTURE OF AT LEAST THREE OF THE CAREERS LISTED THAT YOU CAN CUT OUT AND PASTE IN THE BOX.

WRITE IT DOWN:

What career would you like to learn more about?

Why do you think you might be good in that career field?

_____

_____

_____

_____

_____

_____

_____

_____

_____

I CAN BE...!

WHAT IS A CAREER?

Whatever career you choose, make sure you have what it takes to do it well! Name some careers of family members, TV characters, people you've seen on posters, and of people you see at places you like to go. Our careers are:

[Paste your pictures here:]

Our five letters are: __ __ __ __ __

AT HOME: Pick a career that interests you the most and find out more about it. What does it take to do it well?

I will find out more about a career in _____

MATERIALS:

✓ Pencil
✓ Map of the U.S.
✓ Coloring Materials
✓ Paper

Using the map as a guide, list the states where various members of your family were born. Under each state, write the person's name and year he or she was born. Go back as far as you can, when writing down your family members. Be sure to include your parents, grandparents and their families.

WRITE IT DOWN:

Write a short letter asking a family member to tell you more about your family history. Tell them why you think it's important to know about your family.

_____
_____
_____
_____
_____
_____
_____
_____
_____
_____
_____
_____
_____

ME AND MY FAMILY

Harambee Time #7

STEPS TO TAKE:

Write the words that come to your mind when you hear the word FAMILY.

_____   _____
_____   _____
_____   _____
_____   _____

How many people in your family live with you? _____

Who do you spend the most time with? _____

What do you like to do with your family? _____

How do you help out in the family? _____

Write the name, address, and phone number of a family member that can help you find out more about family members that are no longer living.

_____
_____
_____

NAMES WE CALL OURSELVES

The names we call ourselves should tell us where we live and where our roots are.

MATERIALS:

✓ Pencil

✓ Paper

STEPS TO TAKE:

Write a poem about the names we call ourselves using the following format or one of your own if you prefer.

On a separate piece of paper, draw a picture of your good-looking self!

WRITE IT DOWN:

Write about a friend of yours that has roots in a country or continent different from yourself.

_____

_____

_____

_____

_____

_____

_____

_____

_____

_____

_____

_____

I am _____

    (your name)

I am _____

    (name of ethnic group)

because I live in

_____

    (country)

And my roots are in

_____

(country or continent)

I am/have

_____

_____

(2 words describing physical appearance)

I am

_____

_____

(two words describing positive qualities)

I like to _____

_____

_____

(three things you like to do)

My family _____

    (something about your family)

and I am proud to be an _____

    (name of ethnic group)

READ YOUR POEM TO THE GROUP!!!

MATERIALS

✓ *The Best Face of All*
✓ Coloring Materials
✓ Pencil

STEPS TO TAKE:

Read the book, *The Best Face of All.*

Choose a nose, mouth, skin color, hair style and eyes that are most like yours and draw yourself below. Then think of two friends that look different from yourself. Draw them also. Call the picture "My Friends Come In All Colors"

WRITE IT DOWN:

Write about a time that you were teased because of the color of your skin or the shape or size of your nose or lips. How did it make you feel? What did you do about it?

_____
_____
_____
_____
_____
_____
_____
_____
_____
_____
_____
_____

LET'S TALK ABOUT IT

Are people pretty or ugly because of their skin color?

How did we become so many different colors?

What are some of the negative names we call each other because of our skin color? Why do we do that?

Do you like to be teased about your skin color or other physical traits you were born with?

Name some people that some of the "faces" in the book remind you of.

MATERIALS

✓ Lessons video
✓ Coloring Materials
✓ Pencil

STEPS TO TAKE:

Watch the 45-minute video *Lessons From History* with Dr. Jawanza Kunjufu. Listen closely to the rap song "The Crown" at the end of the tape. Name one thing you learned about African American history from listening to the song. Write your own rap song about feeling proud of who you are or draw a picture of something that makes you proud of your history and culture.

WRITE IT DOWN:

Write about a time that you learned something about your roots that made you feel proud.

_____
_____
_____
_____
_____
_____
_____
_____
_____
_____

LESSONS VIDEO WITH
DR. JAWANZA KUNJUFU

LET'S TALK ABOUT IT

What did you learn from this video?

_____

What is your most important decision?

_____

What is the difference between a natural high and an artificial high?

_____

Why is it important to know our history?

_____

MATERIALS (HG)

✓ Pencil

✓ Coloring Materials

STEPS TO TAKE:

Use the words in the map of Africa below to complete the sentences below. Hint: The region of the continent in which you will find the missing words is written after each sentence.

ADD COLOR AND STYLE TO YOUR MAP TO SHOW THE GREATNESS OF AFRICA!!!

WRITE IT DOWN:

Write a paragraph that starts with "I'm glad I know that about Africa..." Where did you learn most of what you know about Africa?

_____

_____

_____

_____

_____

_____

_____

_____

_____

_____

_____

_____

_____

_____

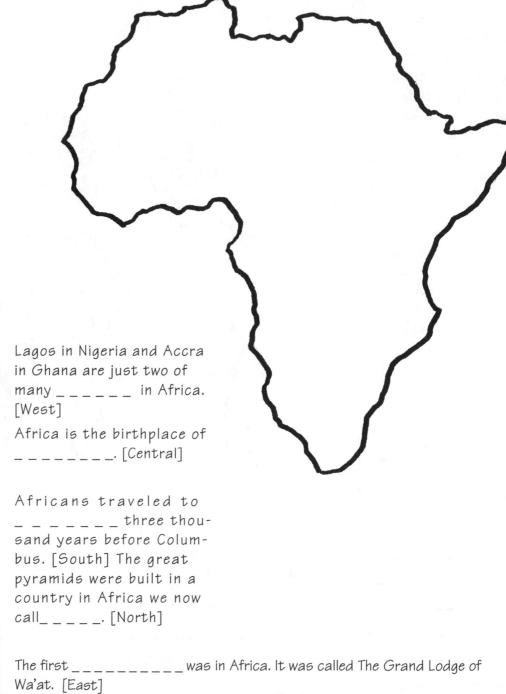

Lagos in Nigeria and Accra in Ghana are just two of many _ _ _ _ _ _ in Africa. [West]

Africa is the birthplace of _ _ _ _ _ _ _ _. [Central]

Africans traveled to _ _ _ _ _ _ _ three thousand years before Columbus. [South] The great pyramids were built in a country in Africa we now call_ _ _ _ _. [North]

The first _ _ _ _ _ _ _ _ _ _ was in Africa. It was called The Grand Lodge of Wa'at. [East]

An African man named _ _ _ _ _ _ _ _ was the father of medicine. He also drew the plans for the first pyramid. [East]

MATERIALS (HG)

✓ *Lessons From History*
✓ *Coloring Materials*
✓ *Poster Board*

STEPS TO TAKE:

Working in your Harambee group, pick one of the four topics listed and design a poster with pictures about your topic. Use the book *Lessons From History* (pages 1 -12) and others for more ideas. When you present your posters to the class, be sure to use the chant "**EGYPT IS IN AFRICA!**"

WRITE IT DOWN:

How would it be to be King Tut, the Egyptian boy king? Write about what might happen during a day in his life.

_____
_____
_____
_____
_____
_____
_____
_____
_____
_____
_____

EGYPT IS IN AFRICA!

Egypt is the place where civilization reached its highest level of achievement a long time ago. **Egypt is in Africa!**

Egypt is known for many things. Some of those things are listed below:

MATERIALS

✓ Pencil

We call this The African Triangle because it shows how people of African descent are in all of these places. When Africans were taken from their homeland, they went to South America and the islands of the Caribbean.

STEPS TO TAKE:

Unscramble the letters in each country to learn a name of a place where many people of African descent now live.

WRITE IT DOWN:

What do African American people have in common with people who live in other parts of the world but have their roots in Africa?

_____

_____

_____

_____

_____

_____

_____

_____

_____

_____

_____

Who can point to the country we live in?

The Caribbean

This country is the home of the great reggae superstar Bob Marley.

— — — — — —

South America

This country is known for Capoeira, a form of martial arts developed by Africans. The language spoken is Portuguese.

— — — — — —

United States of America

This state is a place where many African Americans traveled to looking for jobs and a better life after slavery ended.

— — —   — — — —

Africa

This is the country in which Alex Haley, the author of the book *Roots*, found his family.

— — — — —

FREEDOM FIGHTERS

MATERIALS (HG)

✓ *Lessons From History*

✓ *Pencil*

STEPS TO TAKE:

Read pages 24-27 in the book, *Lessons From History*. Working in Harambee groups, write a little skit about Freedom Fighting using the information on pages 24-27 or the freedom fighters on pages 49, 50, 51, 52, 53 or 54. Many of us are now learning that African people who were taken as slaves resisted slavery in many ways.

WRITE IT DOWN:

How do you think it would feel to be a slave? Why is it important to know that Africans resisted slavery?

_____

_____

_____

_____

_____

_____

_____

_____

_____

_____

_____

_____

_____

What does **resist** mean? _____

Main Characters

Props (such as knives, boats, books, etc.)

The Script (the things the actors will say)

_____

_____

_____

_____

_____

_____

_____

_____

_____

_____

SITTING IN THE FRONT: A Right, A Privilege, A Responsibility

STEPS TO TAKE:

Select group members to act out the following skit. The characters needed are: Rosa Parks, Bus Driver, Policeman, Passengers. Arrange chairs as if they are seats on a bus with one seat for the bus driver and the rest of the seats (no more than 16) for the passengers. Have everybody take their places, leaving one front-row seat empty. Rosa Parks is to walk toward the bus with a heavy bag. She is very tired after a hard day at work where she sews clothes. She gets on the bus and after paying her money, sits in the first and only seat which happens to be in the front of the bus.

WRITE IT DOWN:

What is a right? What is a privilege? What is a responsibility?

How did African Americans earn the right to sit in the front of the bus? How does that make you proud of freedom fighters like Rosa Parks?

_____

_____

_____

_____

_____

Bus Driver: Go to the back of the bus!

Rosa Parks: I'm tired and I'm not going to the back of the bus!

Bus Driver: If you don't go to the back of the bus, I'm going to call the police!

Rosa Parks: Then call them!

Bus Driver (picks up imaginary phone): Police, police, this colored lady won't go to the back of the bus!

(**Police Officer** boards the bus and stands over **Rosa Parks**.)

Bus Driver: This colored lady won't go to the back of the bus.

Policeman: Colored lady, go to the back of the bus!

Rosa Parks: I'm not going to the back of the bus!

Policeman: If you don't go to the back of the bus, I'm going to take you to jail.

Rosa Parks: Then take me! (**Police Officer** takes **Rosa Parks** off the bus.)

Entire class: If you miss me from the back of the bus and you can't find me nowhere, just come on up to the front of the bus and I'll be riding up there!

Note: After Rosa Parks went to jail, with the help of Dr. Martin Luther King, Jr., African Americans boycotted the buses in Montgomery, Alabama. For over one year, people walked and took cabs until the law changed because the bus company was losing a lot of money. African Americans were finally able to sit wherever they wanted on the buses.

LET'S TALK ABOUT IT

What is a boycott? Why was it important to boycott the buses?

Was Rosa Parks a freedom fighter? Why is it good to sit in the front of class or at a special event?

MATERIALS (HG)

✓ *Lessons From History*

✓ Index Cards

✓ Pencil

LET'S TALK ABOUT IT!

Why is history important? What does relevant mean?

How is history relevant to our everyday lives?

How can we use these lessons learned in our everyday lives?

WRITE IT DOWN:

How can these lessons help us get rid of some of the problems in our neighborhoods like crime, violence and drugs?

Why is it so important to know our history?

_____

_____

_____

_____

_____

_____

_____

_____

_____

_____

_____

_____

STEPS TO TAKE:

Give each Harambee Group 10 index cards. Using pages 92, 94, 96, 97, 98, 100 in the book *Lessons From History*, pick one sentence from the history fact (the first paragraph on each page) and write it on an index card. Then write the lesson learned (IN YOUR OWN WORDS) on another index card. Find four more history facts and lessons learned and write them on the cards.

Study the cards and then play a game of Concentration by turning all the cards over on the blank side and taking turns by trying to match the history fact with the lesson learned. On each turn, a player is only allowed to turn over 2 cards. If they don't match, they are turned back over and the next player has a turn. You can decorate the blank side of the card by writing your Harambee Group name in bright colors.

History Fact:

Lesson Learned: _____

History Fact:

Lesson Learned: _____

History Fact:

Lesson Learned: _____

History Fact:

Lesson Learned: _____

History Fact:

Lesson Learned: _____

SWITCH! Play with other Harambee Group's cards.

My History is no mystery!!!

MATERIALS (HG)

✓ Pencil
✓ Index Cards

STEPS TO TAKE:

Who can name a living African American who is doing great things in literature, science, politics, business, and education? Working in Harambee Groups, write your group name on one side of 10 index cards. On the other side, write the name of the living leaders below on each card. Refer to the section **"Something You Should Know"** for information on great African Americans.

WRITE IT DOWN:

Who is a living leader in your community that makes you proud? What great things would you like to do for your community when you grow up?

_____
_____
_____
_____
_____
_____
_____
_____
_____
_____
_____
_____

Use the cards to play a Relay Race with another Harambee Group. Each player tapes the card to a wall that has all 5 categories posted (Literature, Science, Business, Politics, and Education).

The object of the game is for your team to tape the cards under the correct category which each leader belongs. Be sure to tape the card so that the side with the Harambee Group name is showing! In this game, everyone is a winner!

MATERIALS

✓ Pencil
✓ *Lessons From History*
✓ Coloring Materials

STEPS TO TAKE:

There are many groups of people in America that have their own culture. Can you name any? Today, we are going to learn about African American culture.

Unscramble the words of the pictures below. They are all a part of African American culture. All the words can be found in the book *Lessons From History* in the chapter called Black Culture (pages 73 - 88).

A part of African American style is to be colorful. Bring some culture to the pictures above with crayons, markers, paint.

Use your KUUMBA (creativity).

WRITE IT DOWN:

Write about some part of your culture that makes you proud.

_____

_____

_____

_____

BLACK CULTURE

What is culture?

KSHDIIA __ __ __ __ __ __ __

RUCHHC __ __ __ __ __ __

__ __ __ , __ __ __ __ __ , __ __ __ __ __ __ __ __ __ __ __ __ __
DER, LCBAK, NAD RGENE LGAF

ZWANAKA __ __ __ __ __ __ __

ARHABEME __ __ __ __ __ __ __ __
(Let's Pull Together!)

ZAZJ __ __ __ __

LET'S TALK ABOUT IT

If there was a Culture Day and you were supposed to wear clothing, bring foods, and get on stage and perform from your culture, what would you wear, bring, and perform?

MATERIALS

✓ Pencil

LET'S TALK ABOUT IT

Is Black English bad? When is it important to speak Standard English? When is it okay to speak Black English or other dialects?

FOR FUN -

Find a television program that has a character that speaks Black English. Listen to a little, turn it off and see if you can "translate" into Standard English. With this skill, you can go far!!!

WRITE IT DOWN:

What did you like about this lesson? How will it be helpful to you to be able to understand and speak both Black English and Standard English?

STEPS TO TAKE:

Answer these questions:

What is a dialect?

_____

_____

_____

What is Black English?

_____

_____

_____

Who can you think of on television that speaks in Black English?

_____

_____

_____

Play this game. Pick someone to say each sentence and have them pick someone to answer the following questions: Is the sentence Black English or Standard English? Can you say it in the other dialect?

1. He be goin' to school lookin' sharp every day!
2. I have some money in my pocket.
3. He don't look good in that shirt.
4. I asked Jabari do he wanna come.
5. What time is it?
6. I'mma do my homework afta' I get somethin' to eat.
7. I am going to meet my friends at the library.
8. I asked Tameka to come with us.
9. Don't be messin' with me!
10. Please leave me alone!

PUBLIC SPEAKING

MATERIALS
✓ Pencil

STEPS TO TAKE:

Plan your own 1 to 2 minute speech on one of the following topics:

- If I was Principal of

_____

(name of your school)

- The Famous Person I Would Like to Meet Most

_____

- When I Grow Up ...

_____

Everyone is to give their speech to the group.

_____

_____

_____

Give comments to each speaker on how well they possess the quali-ties listed.

WRITE IT DOWN:

What topic do you feel so strongly about that you would speak to one thousand people about it? What would you say?

_____

_____

_____

_____

_____

_____

Why is it important to be able to speak well in public? _____

_____

_____

Who are some public speakers you admire? _____

_____

_____

Name some careers in which it is important to be a good public speaker?

_____

_____

ACTIVITY

Match the quality of a good public speaker with the right picture.

Keeps good eye contact
with audience

Looks around room to
look at **everyone** in the audience

Speaks loudly without screaming

Stands straight and tall

Keeps topic interesting or exciting

MATERIALS (HG)

✓ Music cassette
✓ Cassette Player

LET'S TALK ABOUT IT

Many times we sing a song without thinking about what we're actually saying. Let's listen to a song (a tape someone has or the next song to come on the radio). **Recite, do not sing,** as much of the song as you can. What is the song about? Try it with two more songs. What popular songs can you name that are about something positive?

WRITE IT DOWN:

What is the name of your favorite song? What do you like about it? What is the song about? If you wrote a song, what would it be about? Try writing some of the lyrics (words) to the song.

_____

_____

_____

_____

_____

MUSIC ...THE RADIO

STEPS TO TAKE:

Working in Harambee Groups, think of two songs that everyone in the group likes. Write them down on the lines below:

1.. _____

2. _____

Your teacher or counselor will ask you to talk about the various messages the songs give as it relates to one of the topics below:

1) Being in Love
2) Where to Go to Have Fun
3) Sharing and Working with Others
4) Family
5) Money

Pick members of the group to do the following:

REPORTER
(reports back to
the large group)

_____
(Student's Name)

RECORDER
(takes notes
while the
group is talking)

_____
(Student's Name)

ILLUSTRATOR
(draws pictures
of things the
group talks about)

_____
(Student's Name)

TIMEKEEPER
(reminds the
group how much
time they have)

_____
(Student's Name)

HOW I SPEND MY TIME

MATERIALS

✓ Pencil

STEPS TO TAKE:

Let's see if you can write down everything you did in the last 24 hours. Make sure at least one of the days for which you <u>monitor</u> your time is a weekend (or non-school day). Use the following words to describe what you did within each box. Write the word in each box for each hour of the day.

* Sleep

* School

* TV

* Playing

* Music

* On the Phone

* House Chores

* Personal Hygiene

* Family Time

* Studying

* Traveling

* Group Clubs

LET'S TALK ABOUT IT

How do you spend your time before school? After school? On weekends?

Time	Yesterday's Date	Today's Date	Tomorrow's Date (I'm going to do better.)	Next Day (I'm trying harder.)
7:00 am				
8:00				
9:00				
10:00				
11:00				
12:00 noon				
1:00 p.m.				
2:00				
3:00				
4:00				
5:00				
6:00				
7:00				
8:00				
9:00				
10:00	(By now, you should	be asleep!)		
11:00 - 6:00 am				

Notes:

_____

_____

_____

_____

_____

_____

_____

WRITE IT DOWN

I need to spend more time _____ I need to spend less time _____.

I didn't realize I spend so much time _____.

I didn't realize I spend so little time _____.

How much time do you spend working on your goals? _____

{Remember the goal you set for Harambee Time # 5!}

MATERIALS

✓ Pencil

STEPS TO TAKE:

How many hours of television do you watch in a day?

WRITE IT DOWN:

What would you change about your favorite television program to make it a better show from which others can learn to "do the right thing?"

_____
_____
_____
_____
_____
_____
_____
_____
_____
_____
_____
_____
_____
_____
_____

AT HOME - Use the same list to watch a show with your family and talk about what you see.

TELEVISION

In the space below, write down the name of your three favorite TV programs.

My Favorite TV Shows   The Characters on My Show

_____   _____

_____   _____

_____   _____

What are two of your favorite commercials?

_____
_____
_____

Which show has taught you something about each of the following areas?

Write down the name of the show next to what it taught you.

IMPORTANT VALUES

What You Should Eat _____

The Importance of School _____

Family Time _____

The Importance of
Getting Along Well
With Others _____

How to Spend Money _____

MATERIALS: (HG)

✓ Pencil

LET'S TALK ABOUT IT

What do people who kill others and use or sell drugs value the most? How do we teach positive values? Does TV always teach good values? Give examples.

What are the three things you value the most?

1. _____
2. _____
3. _____

WRITE IT DOWN:

Which values do you have that will make you a better person? How?

_____
_____
_____
_____
_____
_____
_____
_____
_____

Write your answers to the following:

1. My Favorite Place to Go _____
2. Something I Would Like to Buy _____
3. Something I Do Well _____
4. What I Like to Do Most _____
5. The Most Important Thing I Own _____
6. Someone Famous I'd Like to Meet _____

MAKE UP YOUR OWN

What is a value? _____
_____

STEPS TO TAKE:

Take turns asking each group member at least one of the following questions. Fill in the blanks by using the answers to the questions above.

Question # 1 - If you make a lot of money _____3_____ing, should you spend it all on ___2_____ or save it so you know you will always be able to _____4_____?

Question # 2 - Would you give _____6_____ your ___5_____ if he or she asked for it? Why or why not?

Question # 3 - Can you think of a way to make money ____3___ing?

Question # 4 - Would your family want to ___4___ or go to ___1___ together?

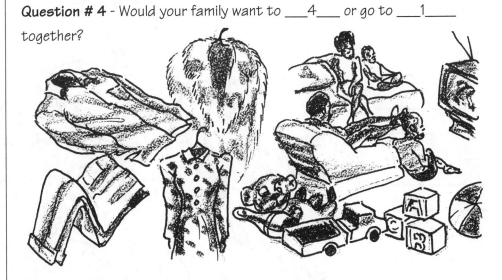

_____
_____
_____
_____

ADVERTISING IMAGES

MATERIALS:
- ✓ Magazines
- ✓ Pencil

ACTIVITY:

Look through magazines and find two ads you consider interesting. What product is being sold? What is the attention grabber? What do you like about the ad? Think of something you really like and create an ad for it. What is the attention grabber in your ad? How do the ads you like affect what you do and what you want to buy?

WRITE IT DOWN:

If you could, what commercials would you remove from television and why? What's your favorite attention grabber? What is your favorite billboard and why?

_____
_____
_____
_____
_____
_____
_____
_____
_____
_____
_____
_____

Harambee Time #25

STEPS TO TAKE:

Answer the following questions:

What is advertising? _____

What is the purpose of advertising? _____

Where do we see and hear ads? _____

What are some your favorite commercials?

Think of at least three of your favorites and write down the name of the product being advertised.

_____
_____
_____

Why do you like these commercials? _____

What grabs your attention for each one? _____

What do you think is being advertised in the ad below?

AAI copyright 1993   40

SCHOOL!!

MATERIALS: (HG)
✓ Pencil

STEPS TO TAKE:

Use the pictures and the scrambled words as clues to complete the phrases below.

Working in Harambee Groups, after you un-scramble the words, discuss your answers and use them to con-vince others how im-portant school is.

Choose one of the fol-lowing ways to do so:

*Write a rap song or poem.
*Create a commercial.
*Prepare a speech.
*Design a poster.

Have you ever heard anyone being teased for doing well in school?

JUST SOME OF THE <u>BENEFITS</u> OF SCHOOL:

We learn how to _____ [hknit]

We learn about _____ choices. [rreeca]

We are able to get a good _____. [bjo]

We _____ so many interesting people. [teme]

We are better prepared to go to _____. [logecle]

What are some other <u>benefits</u> of school?

_____

_____

_____

WRITE IT DOWN:

Make up a sad story about a child who never realized how important it was to do his/her best in school and what happened when the child dropped out of school at only 14 years of age!

41

ME AND MY FRIENDS

MATERIALS

✓ *Sparkle*

✓ Pencil

ACTIVITY:

Think about two of your friends. Circle all the words below that you would use to describe them.

HELPFUL

SMART

CREATIVE

RESPECTS ELDERS

STAYS OUT OF TROUBLE

LIKES FIGHTING

STUDIES HARD

BORING

A LEADER

Circle all the things that you often do with your friends.

PLAY

FIGHT

READ

WATCH TV

TALK ON THE PHONE

DO HOMEWORK

GO TO THE MOVIES

PLAY OUTSIDE

PLAY INDOOR GAMES

HELP OTHERS

WRITE IT DOWN:

Write about one of your best friends. What do you like most about this friend? How do you help this friend? What activities do you do together? Do you ever spend time with your friends' family?

STEPS TO TAKE:

Use the book *Sparkle*. Select students to play the parts of: Storyteller, Marsha, Sparkle, Teasing Children.

After the performance:

Why do you think *Sparkle* made friends with Marsha?

Why is it no one else would be friends with Marsha?

Did Marsha's clothes have anything to do with whether she was a nice, friendly, or a mean person?

What qualities do you look for in a person you just met to decide if you want to be that person's friend?

MATERIALS (HG)
✓ Pencil

LET'S TALK ABOUT IT

Read "Steps to Take."

Would a <u>real</u> friend try to get you to do things that are harmful to you and others? Which one of the following ways has a friend ever tried to get you to do something wrong?

1. Knew you wanted to be part of the group.

2. Dared you or bet that you wouldn't do it.

3. Tried to convince you how tough you are.

4. Lied about what could happen to you if you did it.

WRITE IT DOWN:

Write about a time that a friend tried to get you to do something wrong. How did it make you feel? How did you say NO? Why is it important to be able to say NO?

_____
_____
_____
_____
_____
_____
_____
_____
_____

Have you ever wanted to be an actor or actress? Well, here's your chance!

STEPS TO TAKE:
Here are some situations in which you may find yourself with your friends. Acting them out may help you deal with the situation if it really happens! Pick a few and act them out with your group.

*The Train
Your friends want to sneak on the train just for fun. Not only are you not supposed to ride the trains at all, but your mother also left you in charge of your little brother.

* Skipping School
At lunch, two of your friends tell you they are going to sneak out of school and play basketball. They tell you if you don't come, you're a chump.

*Lying About Homework
After school, you always go home and do your homework. Today, one of your friends tries to persuade you to leave your books at school and tell your parents you forgot them so you won't have to do any homework.

*Stealing Bikes
Two of your best friends have decided to steal some bicycles. They swear that you will not get in trouble if you do it, too.

*The Wine Bottle
Your best friend was walking down the street and found an unopened bottle of wine. He brings it to you so that you all can just "see what it's like". What do you do?

MATERIALS

✓ Pencil

LET'S TALK ABOUT IT

Today, we are going to learn about values that will help us live together better. They are called **THE NGUZO SABA** (n-**goo**-zo **sah**-bah). Nguzo Saba means seven principles. The Nguzo Saba is celebrated during **KWANZAA** from December 26 - January 1st, but we can practice them all year round!

STEPS TO TAKE:

Match each principle to the picture that shows people practicing it. Work together to get the job done!

WRITE IT DOWN:

Pick one of the seven principles and write about how you have practiced it in your life.

_____
_____
_____
_____
_____
_____
_____
_____
_____
_____
_____
_____

THE NGUZO SABA

① UMOJA -
[oo-**mo**-jah] -
UNITY

② KUJICHAGULIA -
[Koo-jee-chah-goo-**lee**-ah]
SELF-DETERMINATION

③ UJIMA -
[**oo**-jee-mah]
COLLECTIVE WORK
AND RESPONSIBILITY

④ UJAMAA -
[**oo**-jah-mah]
COOPERATIVE ECONOMICS

⑤ NIA -
[**nee**-ah]
PURPOSE

⑥ KUUMBA -
[kuh-**um**-bah]
CREATIVITY

⑦ IMANI -
[ee-**mah**-nee]
FAITH

MATERIALS

✓ Pencil

LET'S TALK ABOUT IT

How can we use Kuumba to keep our community clean and make it even more beautiful than before?

Think of a project you can do to make the community more beautiful.

WRITE IT DOWN:

Write about how the community looked after your group completed the project. How did the community members feel? How did it make you feel? How will you continue to keep your community clean and beautiful?

_____
_____
_____
_____
_____
_____
_____
_____
_____
_____
_____
_____
_____
_____
_____

KUUMBA MEANS CREATIVITY

Kuumba is the sixth principle of The Nguzo Saba and it means creativity - **to do always as much as we can in the way we can, in order to leave our community more beautiful than we** <u>inherited</u> **it.**

Some ideas are:

*Pick up trash.

*Get some recycling trash cans for paper, glass, and aluminum cans. Empty them often.

*Paint a mural on a wall. Get permission first from the owner of the building and get an artist to help.

*Plant some flowers or trees.

*Start a grass-cutting business.

*Start a NO LITTERING <u>campaign</u>.

Our class project is:

_____
_____
_____
_____

MATERIALS (HG)

✓ *Carla and Annie*

✓ *Pencil*

As a group, read pages 1 - 8, Take turns reading aloud.

WRITE IT DOWN

How would the story have been different if you wrote it?

If you have a close friend that is a different race than you are, write about how you enjoy learning about each other's culture.

Write about the things you have learned about the music, foods, language, history, etc.

Read the rest of the story and continue the discussion.

_____

_____

_____

_____

_____

_____

_____

_____

_____

_____

_____

_____

_____

_____

CARLA AND ANNIE

LET'S TALK ABOUT IT

1. What did Annie say to Carla that made her sad? Why?

2. If Carla knew more about her culture and history, would Annie's comments have upset her so much?

3. With the information you have about your race, culture and history, what would you have said to Annie if you were Carla?

MATERIALS

✓ Coloring Materials

WRITE IT DOWN:

When you grow up, what things will you do that will make you a man or a woman?

STEPS TO TAKE:

Put a square around all the words that come to your mind when you hear the word MAN.

Circle all the words that come to your mind when you hear the word WOMAN.

LET'S TALK ABOUT IT

Who are some men you admire?

Why?

Who are some women you admire?

Why?

_____
_____
_____
_____
_____
_____
_____
_____
_____
_____
_____
_____
_____
_____
_____

Sensitive

Pretty

Good

Hard-worker

Business Person

Head Of Household

Hairdresser

Doctor

Nurse

Teacher

Handsome

Drug Dealer

Construction Worker

Police

Parent

Do Not Cry

Barber

Strong

Good Driver

Scientist

Weak

Smart

Nice

ANSWER KEY

Harambee Time #11

1. cities
2. humanity
3. America
4. Egypt
5. University
6. Imhotep

Harambee Time #18

1. Dashiki
2. Church
3. red, black, and green flag
4. Kwanzaa
5. Harambee

Harambee Time #25

1. alcohol
2. hair care
3. car
4. alcohol

Harambee Time #29

1. Umoja-3rd box
2. Kujichagulia-2nd box
3. Ujima-6th box
4. Ujamaa-1st box
5. Nia-7th box
6. Kuumba-5th box
7. Imani-4th box

Harambee Time #13

The Caribbean-Jamaica
South America-Brazil
U.S.A.-New York
Africa-Ghana

Harambee Time #20

1. Picture #3
2. Picture #5
3. Picture #1

4. Picture #2
5. Picture #4

Harambee Time #26

1. think
2. career
3. job
4. meet
5. college

SOMETHING YOU SHOULD KNOW.......

Group # 2 - African Countries

Nigeria - This West African country is Africa's most populated country. It is rich with oil.

Kenya - This beautiful East African country is home for the Gikuyu community. Jomo Kenyatta led them to freedom.

Egypt - Civilization began here. It is home of the great pyramids, temples, tombs and King Tut.

Azania - Sometimes called South Africa, it is a country filled with gold and diamonds. We all must remove apartheid, a form of slavery. Azania is the home of Nelson Mandela.

Tanzania - It is an East African country and home of the great former President Julius Nyerere.

Group # 3 - African Communities

Ashanti - A community from Ghana. Many residents work as weavers of beautiful kente cloth and carvers of the Ashanti stool for the king.

Chagga - A community where the children play among others the same age and are taught to be adults by the time they are 15 years old.

Pondo - A community where the children learn self-defense at an early age.

Fanti -A community in West Africa. They pour libation which is pouring a little wine on the ground to honor their dead family members (ancestors)

Ikoma -A community in West Africa. They gather honey to eat and sell.

Group # 4 - Black Colleges

Morehouse College - An all-male school in Atlanta, Georgia. Martin Luther King, Jr. and Spike Lee graduated from Morehouse.

Hampton University - A college in Hampton, Virginia with 4500 students. They have their own radio and TV stations.

Spelman College -An all-female school with nearly 200 students. It's right next door to Morehouse College. Bill and Camille Cosby gave the school $20 million dollars in 1988.

Tuskegee Institute - Founded by Booker T. Washington. They have a pre-veterinarian program (animal doctors). It's in Tuskegee, Alabama.

Howard University - One of the largest Black colleges in the country. It's in Washington, D.C. and has its own medical school.

BLACK EXCELLENCE

LITERATURE

Alex Haley,

wrote the book Roots which went on to be the most watched mini-series in TV history.

Alice Walker,

wrote the book The Color Purple which was later made into a movie. She has written more than 16 books!

EDUCATION

Marva Collins,

opened a school in Chicago in 1975. Almost all of her students do very well, no matter what their background is.

Jawanza Kunjufu,

wrote the book Lessons From History and speaks to teachers all over the country about educating Black children. He has written 11 books in all!

POLITICS

Jesse Jackson,

received more votes (7 million) for each dollar spent than any other candidate in the 1988 Presidential race.

Carol Moseley Braun,

is the first Black woman to become a U.S. Senator.

SCIENCE

Walter Massey,

was once President of the American Association of Science, the world's largest organization of scientists.

Mae Jemison,

is a medical doctor and the first African American female astronaut.

BUSINESS

Herman J. Russell,

founder of H.J. Russell & Co., the largest Black-owned construction firm in the U.S.A. Based in Atlanta, Ga.

Bonnie Marshall,

President of MTB Entertainment. She helps get products of Black-owned companies (such as CrossColours clothing) in movies and department stores.

The SETCLAE Student Profile (3rd Grade)

Instructions

Please answer the following questions on the answer sheet and think real hard about how you really feel before answering each one. THERE ARE NO RIGHT OR WRONG ANSWERS. We want YOUR answers.

Part I

Read each statement or question. If it is true for you, circle the answer "a" on the answer sheet. If it is not true for you, circle the answer "b". Answer every question even if it's hard to decide. (Just think about yourself and what's important to you.) Select only one answer for each question. Write on the answer sheet only.

1. I like to be alone sometimes.   a. Yes   b. No

2. I like to stand in front of the class
    and speak.   a. Yes   b. No

3. When we are cleaning up our classroom,
    if I finish before everybody else, I play.   a. Yes   b. No

4. School will help me to be what
    I want to be.   a. Yes   b. No

5. If I can't think of anything good to say
    about someone, I don't say anything
    at all.   a. Yes   b. No

6. I know what kind of person I want to be
    when I grow up.   a. Yes   b. No

7. I like to play with my favorite toy all
    by myself more than I like to share it
    with others.   a. Yes   b. No

8. If things don't go my way, I get mad.   a. Yes   b. No

9. School is boring most of the time.   a. Yes   b. No

10. Do you speak slang and
    Standard English?   a. Yes   b. No

11. If I don't see a trash can, I throw my
    trash on the ground.   a. Yes   b. No

12. I like participating in special projects
    like science fairs and spelling bees.   a. Yes   b. No

13. When the truth is hard to say,
    I don't say it.   a. Yes   b. No

14. Would you like to be in a family
    other than your own?   a. Yes   b. No

15. My neighborhood is
    a good place to live.   a. Yes   b. No

16. I can get any job I want, if I work at
    it hard enough.   a. Yes   b. No

17. I like being with people that are
    different from me.   a. Yes   b. No

18. I like me!   a. Yes   b. No

19. Do you believe you can have your own
    business when you get older?   a. Yes   b. No

20. There are a lot of people in the world
    more important than I am.   a. Yes   b. No

21. African Americans only do well in
    sports, music, movies , and TV.   a. Yes   b. No

22. If I could, I would make friends with
    races of all people.   a. Yes   b. No

23. In my opinion, most Black people
    are lazy.   a. Yes   b. No

24. I want to be able to speak Standard
    English when I go some places and
    when talking to some people.   a. Yes   b. No

Part II

Read each item carefully. If it is something that is important to you, select "a" on the answer sheet. If it is not important to you (it doesn't really matter or has nothing to do with you), select "b". Take your time and think about it. There are no right or wrong answers. We want to know your feelings.

1. Helping others

    a. Important to Me   b. Not Important to Me

2. What others think of me

    a. Important to Me   b. Not Important to Me

3. Reading

    a. Important to Me   b. Not Important to Me

4. Television

    a. Important to Me   b. Not Important to Me

5. Solving problems by fighting

    a. Important to Me   b. Not Important to Me

6. Learning about my family members - dead & living

    a. Important to Me   b. Not Important to Me

7. Getting along with others

    a. Important to Me   b. Not Important to Me

8. Doing whatever my friends do

    a. Important to Me   b. Not Important to Me

9. Expensive clothes

    a. Important to Me   b. Not Important to Me

10. Doing well in school

    a. Important to Me   b. Not Important to Me

11. Speaking up for myself & my ideas

    a. Important to Me   b. Not Important to Me

12. Being positive most of the time

          a. Important to Me   b. Not Important to Me

13. Life in Africa today

          a. Important to Me   b. Not Important to Me

Part III

Read each statement carefully. Read the choices. Then draw a line under each statement that accurately describes you.

1. If asked to describe my personality to someone I'd never met, I would use statements like:

I'm fun to be around.	I like to get in trouble.
I give up easily.	I'm a good fighter.
I'm a leader.	I'm happy.
I like helping others.	I'm slow.
I'm easily bored.	I'm unhappy.
I'm friendly.	I worry a lot.
I'm popular.	I'm big and bad.
I'm outgoing.	

2. If asked to describe my physical appearance, I would say I am or have

average-looking	too short	too fat
pretty eyes	light-skinned	dark-skinned
nice hair	beautiful/handsome	slim
a head that is too big		lips that are too big
a nose that is too big		

3. Circle one.

         I   a. like   my hair.

                       b. don't like

4. I chose the above answer because my hair is:

short	long	thick	straight
curly	nappy	dark	red
light	natural	braided	mine!

5. Circle one.

I   a. like   my skin color.

                           b. don't like

6. I chose the above answer because my skin is:

                    dark   light   just right

7. Circle the five words that first come to your mind when you hear the word Africa.

slavery	city
Tarzan	jungle
continent	kings and queens
Egypt	pyramids
civilization	savage
homeland	country
wild	monkeys

8. Circle the one that is more important to you. Choose only one!

I like

a. being popular

b. doing well in school

Part IV

Carefully read the following statements and choices for answers. Then pick the answer that is best for you. Circle the letter that is in front of your answer on the answer sheet.

There are NO RIGHT OR WRONG ANSWERS. Choose the answer that is right for YOU.

1. When my friends have fun without me, I
    a. am happy they are having fun.
    b. don't even think about it.
    c. wish they weren't having fun without me.

2. When I hear something negative about a person, I
    a. can't wait to tell someone else.
    b. talk to the person to see how I can help.
    c. try to find out more.

3. When someone says something about me that is not good but is true, I

    a. get upset.

    b. don't want to be around them anymore.

    c. listen and learn from their observations.

    d. say something about them that is not good.

4. When someone laughs at me,

    a. I get upset.

    b. my feelings are hurt.

    c. I laugh with them.

    d. I make a joke of it.

    e. I don't like it.

5. When I am talking to someone, most of the time I look

    a. at their hands.

    b. into their eyes.

    c. at the floor.

    d. all around.

6. How much time do you spend making yourself look good?

    a. no time

    b. very little time

    c. some of the time

    d. all of the time

7. If I had lots of money, I would

    a. be happy all the time.

    b. help others.

    c. need and want more money.

    d. save it.

8. When I play team games, I

    a. like to be the captain.

    b. have fun even if my team loses.

    c. don't like losing.

    d. often get in a fight.

9. When I need help, I

    a. get frustrated.

    b. ask for it.

    c. try to figure it out myself.

10. I pick my friends because
    a. they look good.
    b. they are cool.
    c. we can talk a lot.
    d. they give me things.

11. I am glad I am the race I am.
    a. Yes
    b. No

12. I chose the answer above because
    a. I am proud of it.
    b. I know my history.
    c. it sounds good.
    d. I was taught by my family.
    e. my friends chose the same answer.

13. My favorite musical group or person is _____ because
    a. they play good dancing music.
    b. they sing about good things.
    c. they make good videos.
    d. of the cursing in the songs.
    e. they play nice music to listen to.

14. A boy becomes a man when
    a. he can handle drugs and crime.
    b. he makes a baby.
    c. he takes care of himself and his family.
    d. he can fight.

15. When I can sit wherever I want in class, I sit
    a. in the middle.
    b. in the front.
    c. in the back.

16. When the teacher leaves the room, I
    a. talk.
    b. stop doing my work.
    c. look at who is being out of order.
    d. find something quiet to do once I finish my work.

17. My favorite TV show is _____ because
    a. it's funny.
    b. there's a lot of kissing/fighting.
    c. I like the nice clothes, fancy cars, and pretty houses.
    d. I learn new things from it.
    e. I like the actors.

18. When I want to do something new (like join a sports team), I
    a. ask my parents to get me started.
    b. plan how I will do it.
    c. just think about it real hard.
    d. ask my friends to get me started.

19. When I do poorly on my schoolwork, I
    a. don't really care.
    b. know I tried my best.
    c. know I should try harder.
    d. know it's only because I can't do any better.
    e. know the teacher gave us work that was too hard or boring.

20. If I could change one thing about myself, it would
    be_____.

21. The thing I like most about myself
    is_____.

22. Answering these questions was
    a. very enjoyable.
    b. no big deal.
    c. a good way to take a closer look at my personal development.
    d. a waste of time.

SETCLAE PRONUNCIATION GLOSSARY

Phonics

a-short a   i-long e

e-long a   o-long o

u-long u

Kiswahili

Jambo	Hello
Habari Gani	What is the news?
Njema	Fine
Asante	Thank you
Asante Sana	Thank you very much
Mama	Mother
Baba	Father
Ndada	Sister
Ndugu	Brother
Watoto	Children
Mtoto	Child
Mwalimu	Teacher
Mwanafunzi	Student
Shule	School
Yebo	Yes
La	No
Acha	Stop
Nisamehe	Excuse me
Tafadali	Please
Mzuri	Good
Harambee	Let's pull together
Pamoja Tutashinda	Together we will win
Mzee	Elder
Chakula	Food
Choo	Toilet
Hodi hodi	Hurry
Tutaonana	Goodbye

Moja	One
Mbil	Two
Tatu	Three
Nne	Four
Tano	Five
Sita	Six
Saba	Seven
Nane	Eight
Tisa	Nine
Kumi	Ten

Umoja	Unity
Kujichagulia	Self-determination
Ujima	Collective work and responsibility
Ujamaa	Cooperative Economics
Nia	Purpose
Kuumba	Creativity
Imani	Faith